SO WHAT?

McClelland & Stewart, Inc.
The Canadian Publishers
481 University Avenue
Toronto M5G 2E9

Canadian Cataloguing in Publication Data
Aislin.
The Lawn Jockey
ISBN 0-7710-6519-1
1. Canada—Politics and government—1987–1989—Caricatures and cartoons.*
2. World politics—1987–1989—Caricatures and cartoons. 3. Sports—Caricatures and cartoons. 4. Canadian wit and humour, Pictorial. I. Title.
NC1449.A37A4 1989 741.5′971 C89-094624-8

Other Books by Aislin
Aislin—100 Caricatures (1971)
Hockey Night in Moscow (1972, with Jack Ludwig)
Aislin—150 Caricatures (1973)
The Great Hockey Thaw (1974, with Jack Ludwig)
'Ello, Morgentaler? Aislin—150 Caricatures (1975)
O.K. Everybody Take a Valium! Aislin—150 Caricatures (1977)
L'Humour d'Aislin (1977)
The Retarded Giant (1977, with Bill Mann)
The Hecklers: A History of Canadian Political Cartooning (1979, with Peter Desbarats)
The Year the Expos Almost Won the Pennant (1979, with Brodie Snyder)
Did the Earth Move? Aislin—180 Caricatures (1980)
The Year the Expos Finally Won Something (1981, with Brodie Snyder)
The First Great Canadian Sports Trivia Quiz Book (1981, with Brodie Snyder)
Stretchmarks (1982)
The Anglo Guide to Survival in Quebec (1983, with various Montreal writers)
Tootle: A Children's Story (1984, with John Sarrazin)
Where's the Trough? (1985)
Old Whores (1987)
WHAT'S THE BIG DEAL? Some straightforward questions and answers on free trade (1988, with Rick Salutin)

Printed and bound in Canada

Special thanks to Peter Arsenault, who is a part of all this; Johanne Norchet, for the occasional cedilla; and Charis Wahl, for laughing in all the right places. Also, Mark Harrison at *The Gazette* for putting up with me for thirteen years.

"THE LAWN JOCKEY"

M&S

and other "AISLIN" cartoons . . .

This collection is dedicated to my partner Carol who, over twenty-five years, also became my best friend.

INTRODUCTION

An exceptional novelist absorbs our interest because he or she has mastered technique and has something striking to say. Whether such absorption makes us feel good is beside the point — as is whether the novelist has been fair or compassionate or comprehensive. So it is with Terry Mosher.

Mosher is a great cartoonist because the technique is there in all the exquisite detail of the drawings, but it's detail that underscores and never destroys the message. The drawings are frequently quite subtle but the message never is. It hits you with great force.

You may laugh or feel outraged, but the power of his art ensures that you will not be indifferent. Mosher is an enemy of the pompous and fatuous. Compromise he sees as a virtue better left with Aristotle.

Like all great cartoonists, he responds passionately to what is happening in his world. In his dealings with issues of the day, you always know what side he's on. You know where he stands on the trade deal, on language rights, on censorship, and on the banality of a yuppie's celebration of contemporary Toronto. His expressed ideology is neither left nor right. He's a rare bird, a Canadian anarchist on guard equally against those with power and those aspiring to it.

A book by a cartoonist is to be viewed. So get on with it. Laugh, get angry, appreciate the art. Terry Mosher is one of the best.

Ed Broadbent

FREE TRADE…

AGREED! CANADA WILL CORNER THE NORTH AMERICAN MARKET ON HAND-CARVED HAIDA CHESS PIECES AND BOARDS WHILE THE U.S. CONTROLS OIL…
AISLIN '87
MONTREAL GAZETTE

TWO GREAT CANADIANS...
CANADA IS NOT FOR SALE!
CANADA IS NOT FOR SALE!!
GET BUSY...
AISLIN 87. MONTREAL GAZETTE

Free Trade
The United States of
America
shake
down
will
Canada
continue
to
forever.
Forget this! Peter Murphy.
No. David Peterson.
Very funny! Simon.
HA! HA! U.S. CONGRESS.
This would harm the Italian designers Mila!
And kill my T.V. series? Shelly.
Ronald Reagan
AISLIN '87 MONTREAL GAZETTE

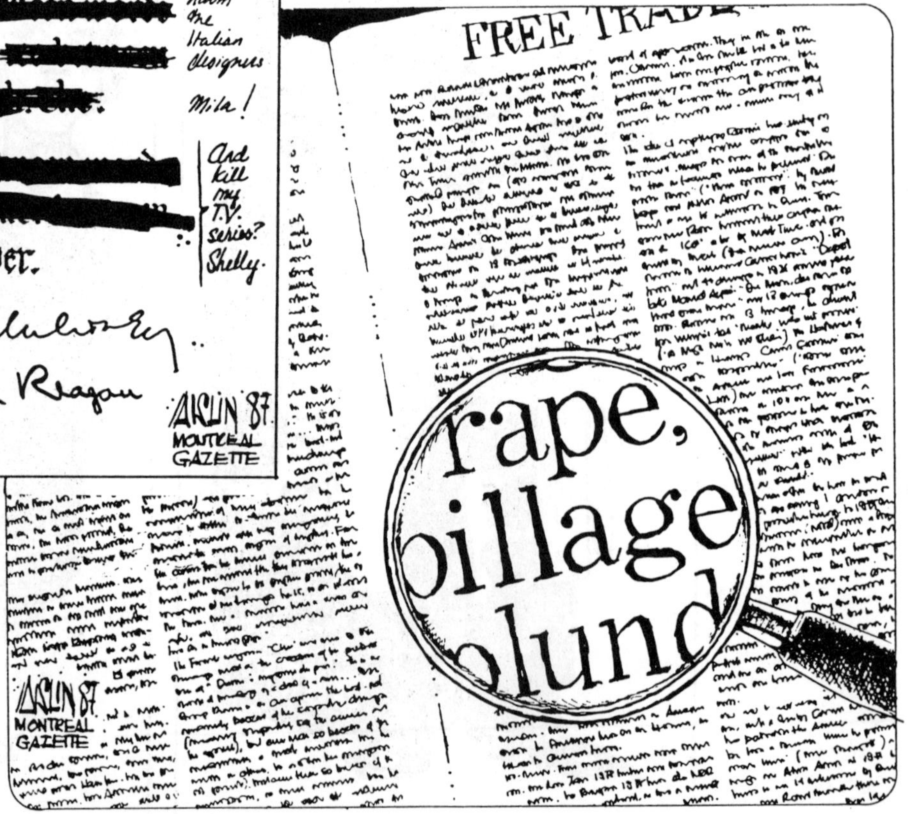

FREE TRADE
rape,
illage
lund
AISLIN 87 MONTREAL GAZETTE

AISLIN '88
MONTREAL
GAZETTE

U.S. GOODS
POUTINE
AISLIN 87.
MONTREAL GAZETTE

NOW REGARDING FREE TRADE WITH CANADA - DIDN'T THIS BRIAN MULORNEY DO SOME WORK FOR US IN THE PAST?
THAT'S RIGHT... SCHEFF-ERVILLE.
AISLIN 88.
MONTREAL GAZETTE

BUT SOMEONE JUST SUGGESTED THAT I COULD POSSIBLY BE REMEMBERED AS CANADA'S WORST-EVER PRIME MINISTER...
NOT A CHANCE, SIR - IF OUR HISTORIANS END UP BEING THE AMERICANS!
AISLIN '88
MONTREAL GAZETTE

WELL, SHORE... I KNOW LOTS ABOUT CANAYDEEYIN CULCHUR... HELL, I EVEN MET PETER ZOWSKI ONCE!
AISLIN 88
MONTREAL GAZETTE

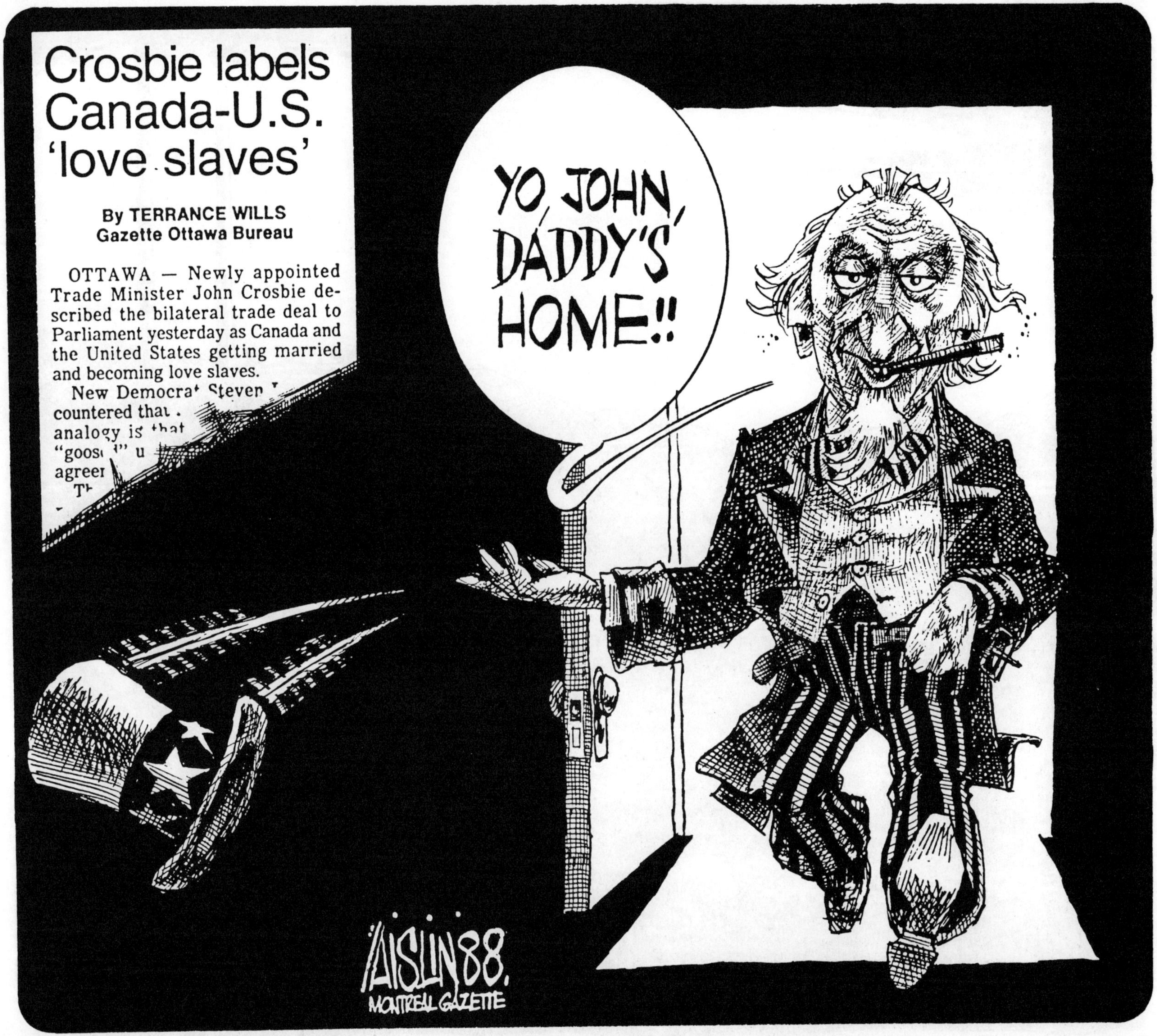
Crosbie labels Canada-U.S. 'love slaves'
By TERRANCE WILLS
Gazette Ottawa Bureau
OTTAWA — Newly appointed Trade Minister John Crosbie described the bilateral trade deal to Parliament yesterday as Canada and the United States getting married and becoming love slaves.
YO, JOHN, DADDY'S HOME!!
AISLIN 88.
MONTREAL GAZETTE

WHY DID WE WANT FREE TRADE WITH THE U.S. IN THE FIRST PLACE?
AISLIN 87
MONTREAL GAZETTE

Don't worry,
Be happy!
AISLIN 88
MONTREAL GAZETTE

Hopes that the annual Caribbean street festival will ease tensions between Blacks and the police.

MONTREAL…

…THE SUSPECTS ARE ARMED AND EXTREMELY DANGEROUS … WANTED FOR QUESTIONING IN CONNECTION WITH AN ASSAULT AND BATTERY, A SEXUAL ASSAULT AND OTHER CHARGES… LAST SEEN IN A BLUE AND WHITE 4-DOOR SEDAN, LICENSE P-80191…
POLICE
DE MONTREAL
84-1
POLICE
84-1
P-80191
AISLIN 87
MTL GAZETTE

Record rainfall causes city-wide flooding.

Le Grand Prix.

Fashionable Outremont types upset by local Orthodox Jews.

The Montreal Jazz Festival.

OLD BREWERY MISSION
...THAT REMINDS ME. NOVEMBER IS COMING... I'LL HAVE TO FIND A COAT.
P.M.'s SUITS COST $2500s
AISLIN '87
MONTREAL GAZETTE

Dorchester Boulevard's name is changed to Boulevard René-Lévesque.

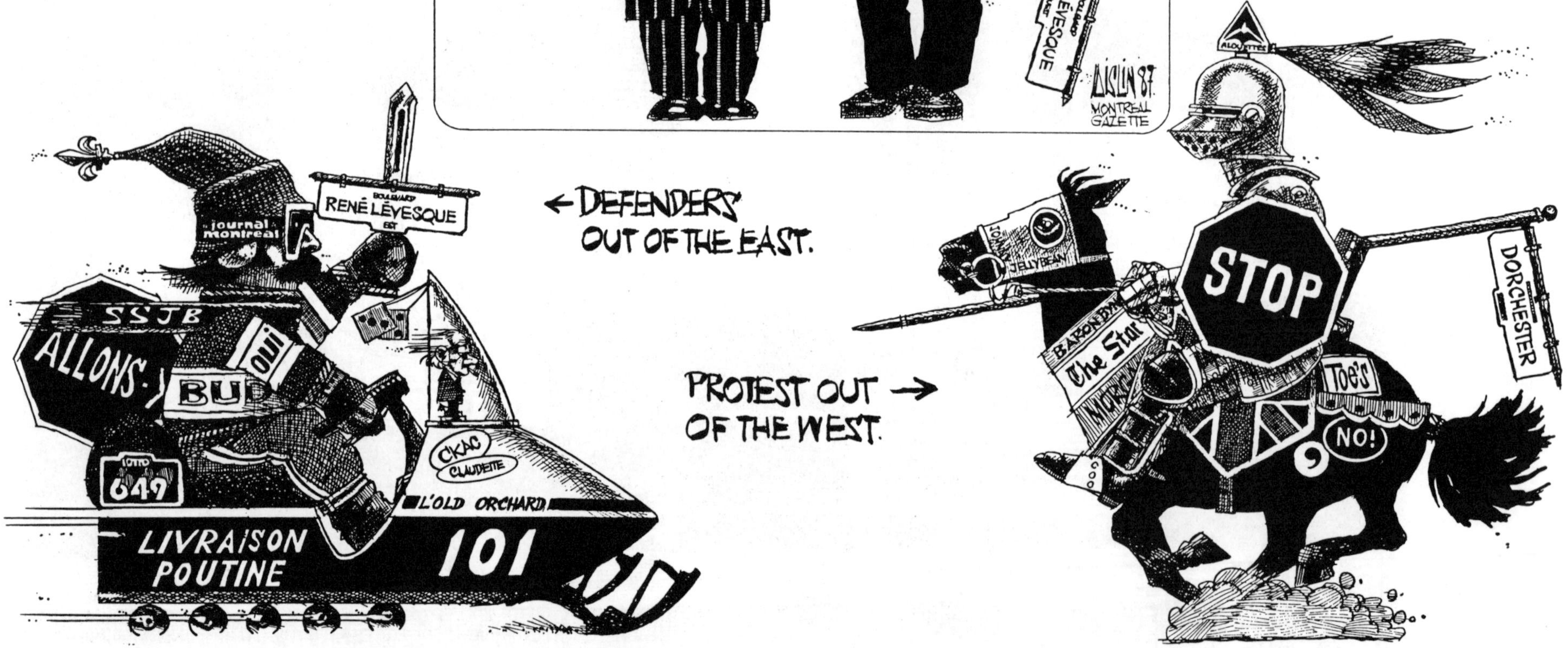

IT'S HARD TO IMAGINE THAT THERE MIGHT EVER BE A BOULEVARD JACQUES PARIZEAU...
MMM... MAYBE A LAKE.
AISLIN 88.
MONTREAL GAZETTE

20
BRILLIANT IDEA, VAL!
MONTREAL GAZETTE

ITEM: CITY BUYS $63,220. PIANO.
CHOPSTICKS!!..
AISLIN 87
MONTREAL GAZETTE

INTERNATIONAL…

AISLIN 88
MONTREAL
GAZETTE

...THEN NANCY, WANTING RON TO BE REMEMBERED WELL IN THE HISTORY BOOKS, PHONED RAISA TO SAY THAT IN DECEMBER NEIMAN-MARCUS WAS HAVING A SALE.
MITTS
SURGICAL GLOVES
AISLIN 88
MONTREAL GAZETTE

DURAC
AISLIN 88
MONTREAL GAZETTE

YOU KNOW, NANCY, IT'D BE NICE TO GO OUT WITH A BANG...
WHY, RON, YOU OLD RASCAL!
I WAS THINKING OF LIBYA, DEAR.
1001 FREE THINGS
AISLIN 83
MONTREAL GAZETTE

WELL, um... GOOD LUCK, FRED!
sigh...
AISLIN 89
MONTREAL GAZETTE
JELLY

GOLL-Y, DAN! ISN'T THIS JUST GREAT? ABSOLUTELY EVERYBODY IS CALLING TO WISH ME WELL...
AISLIN '88
MONTREAL GAZETTE

L.L.Bush
BOOM!
AISLIN '88
MONTREAL GAZETTE

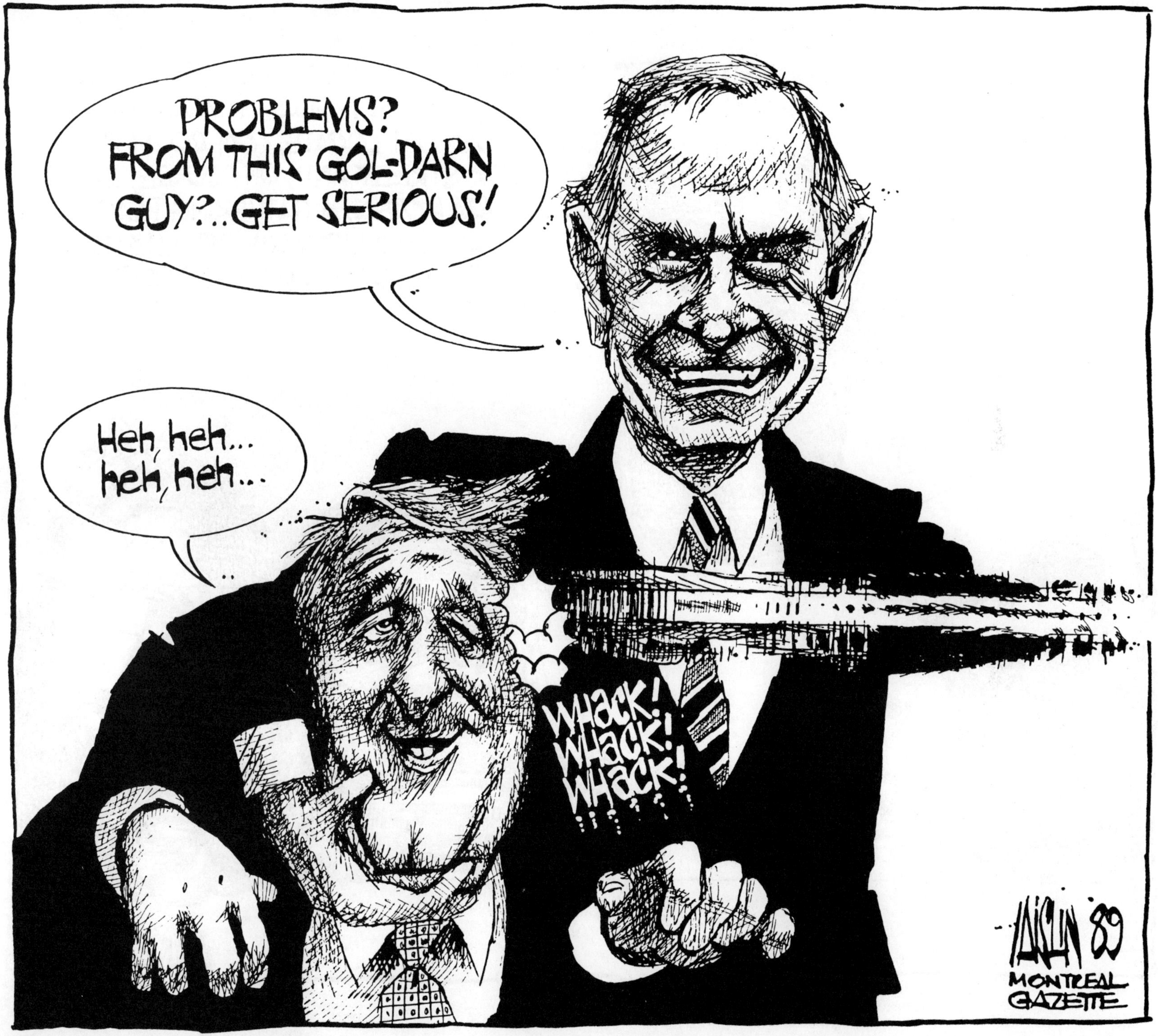
PROBLEMS? FROM THIS GOL-DARN GUY?..GET SERIOUS!
Heh, heh... heh, heh...
WHACK! WHACK! WHACK!
AISLIN '89
MONTREAL GAZETTE

Toronto Summit.

AISLIN 88
MONTREAL GAZETTE
TORONTO'S CHANGED!
YES, I AGREE...WE REALLY HAVE CHANGED!
YES, REALLY AND TRULY!
YUP... BIG CHANGE
AND, DESPITE THOSE LEAFS, WE'VE REALLY CHANGED!
WE'RE KINDA LIKE NEW YORK CITY NOW, EH?
WOW-EE, MILDRED, TRONO'S CHANGED!
WHAD'A CHANGE!
PLUS ÇA CHANGE...
I BEG YOUR PARDON?
←HAMILTON
EX
BERTON DONUTS
Atwood Dairy
We've changed!
SMILE!
IF YOU CAN'T READ THIS, YOU SHOULD BE READING THE SUN!
$!
OSHAWA→

HOW THE WEST WAS LOST...
DON'T PLAY WITH YOUR GUN; PLAY WITH YOUR DICK!
AISLIN 88
MONTREAL GAZETTE

NOW...
AISLIN 88
MONTREAL GAZETTE

Alaska oil spill.

WELL I MUST SAY THAT YOUR BOOK REVIEW IS MOST CERTAINLY A REVOLUTIONARY APPROACH TO LITERARY CRITICISM!
BOOK EDITOR
THE SATANIC VERSES
AISLIN 89
MONTREAL GAZETTE

PERHAPS WE COULD GO BACK TO HARASSING THE AMERICANS?....
SNIP! SNIP! SNIP!
AISLIN 89
MONTREAL GAZETTE

LOOK! A JUMPER!!
NOPE...A SMOKER...
AISLIN 88
MONTREAL GAZETTE

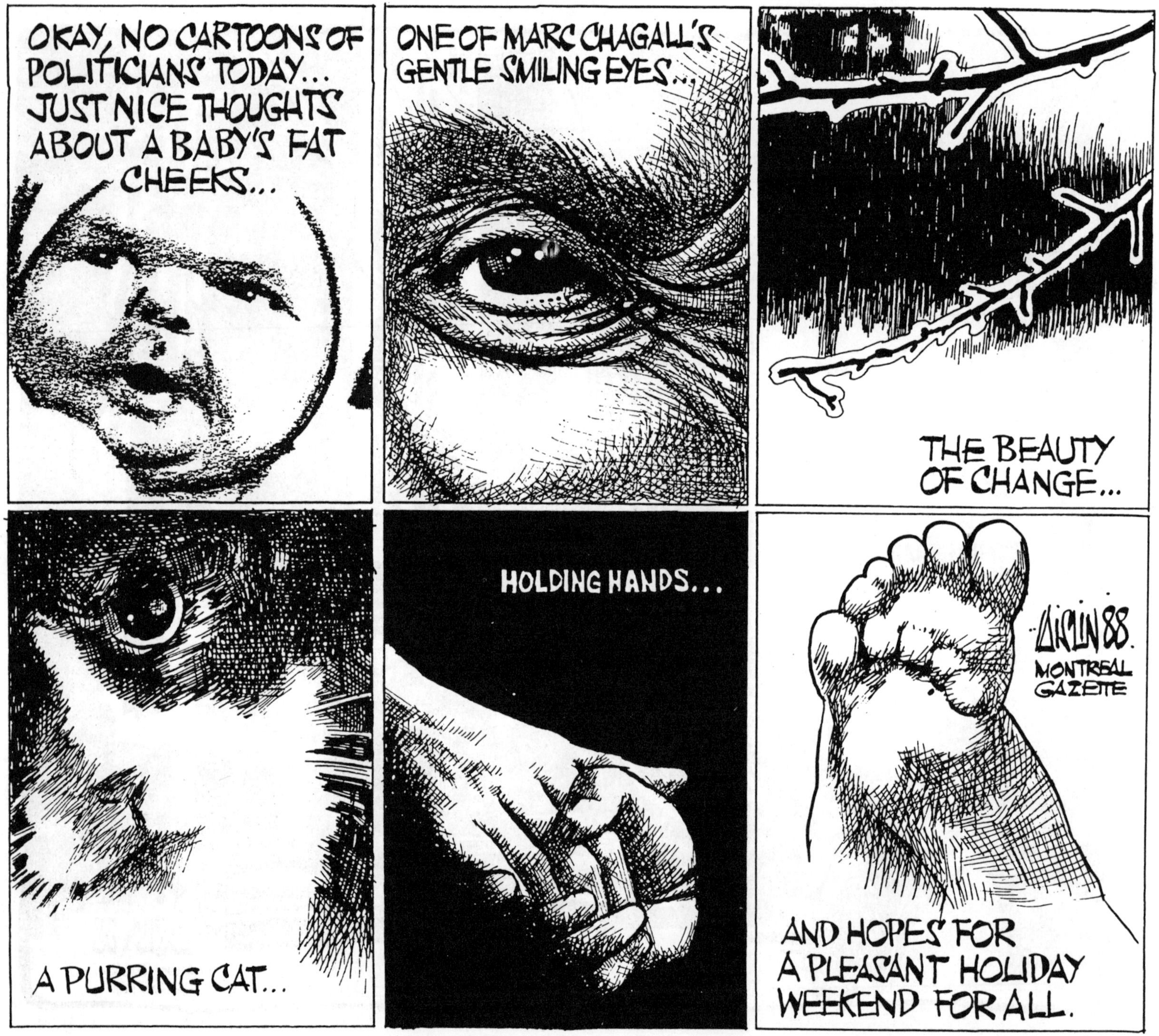
OKAY, NO CARTOONS OF POLITICIANS TODAY... JUST NICE THOUGHTS ABOUT A BABY'S FAT CHEEKS...
ONE OF MARC CHAGALL'S GENTLE SMILING EYES...
THE BEAUTY OF CHANGE...
A PURRING CAT...
HOLDING HANDS...
AISLIN 88.
MONTREAL GAZETTE
AND HOPES FOR A PLEASANT HOLIDAY WEEKEND FOR ALL.

WHAT EVER HAPPENED TO POETRY?...
I DON'T HAVE THAT SOFTWARE.
MONTREAL GAZETTE

TORNADOES, EARTHQUAKES, POWER FAILURES... WHAT'S A YOUNG REVOLUTIONARY TO DO?
SWITCH YOUR JUNK BONDS INTO BLUE-CHIP GOVERNMENT SECURITIES FOR A START...
ALSO, SHORT THE DOLLAR AND LOAD UP ON YEN.
IBM
AISLIN 88.
MONTREAL GAZETTE

The Crash of 1987.

WERE THOSE RUSSIANS OR AMERICANS?
THEY WERE HUMAN BEINGS...
AISLIN 88
MONTREAL GAZETTE

International AIDS Conference held in Montreal

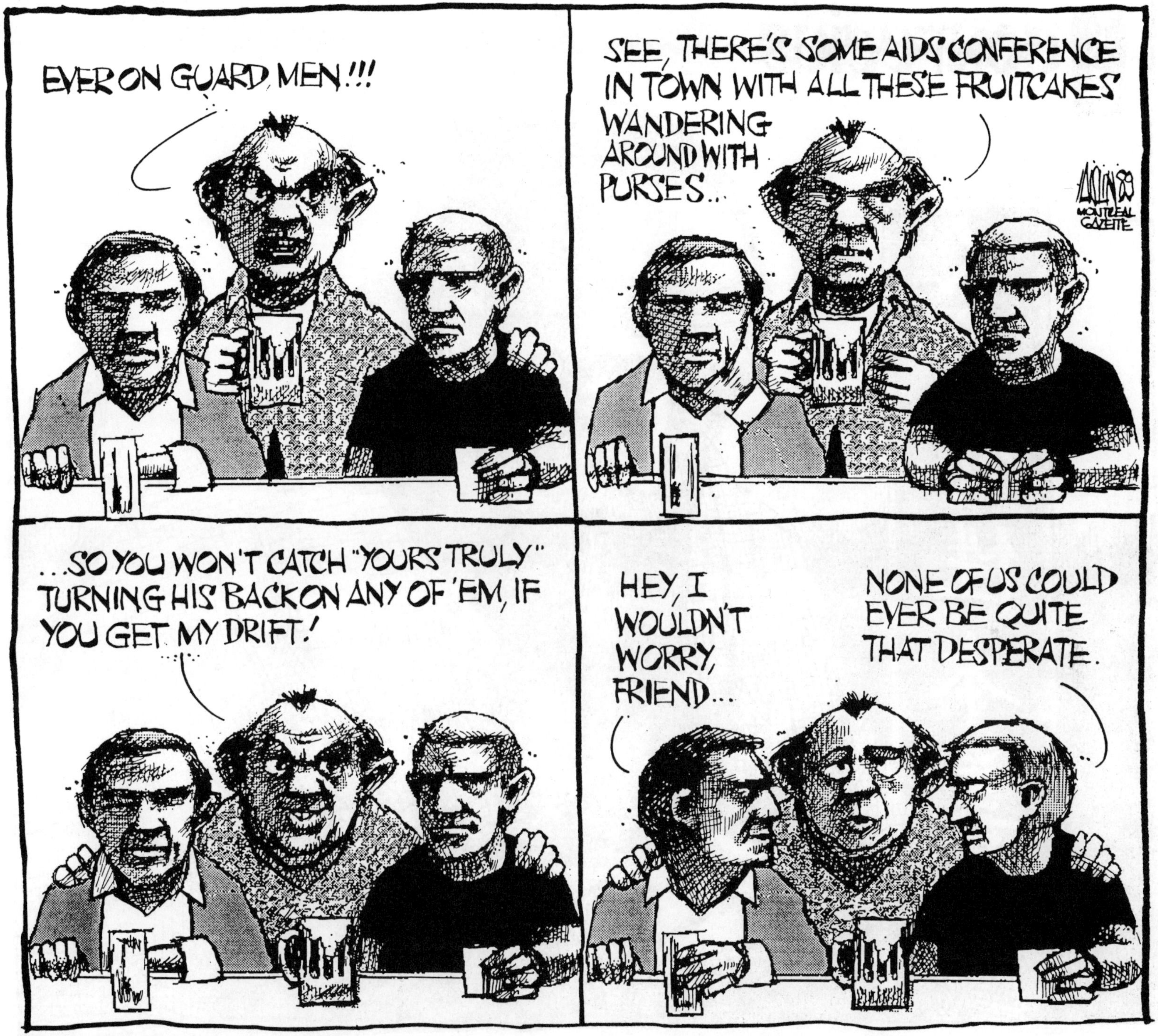

孔子
CONFUCIUS
人自初性本善
MONTREAL GAZETTE

A TRUE CHINESE "MOST-WANTED" POSTER...

DENG XIAO PING, MALE, BORN AUGUST 1904. DESCRIPTION: MUDDLE-HEADED AND SENILE. OCCUPATION: CHINESE DICTATOR. CRIME: MURDER of STUDENTS.

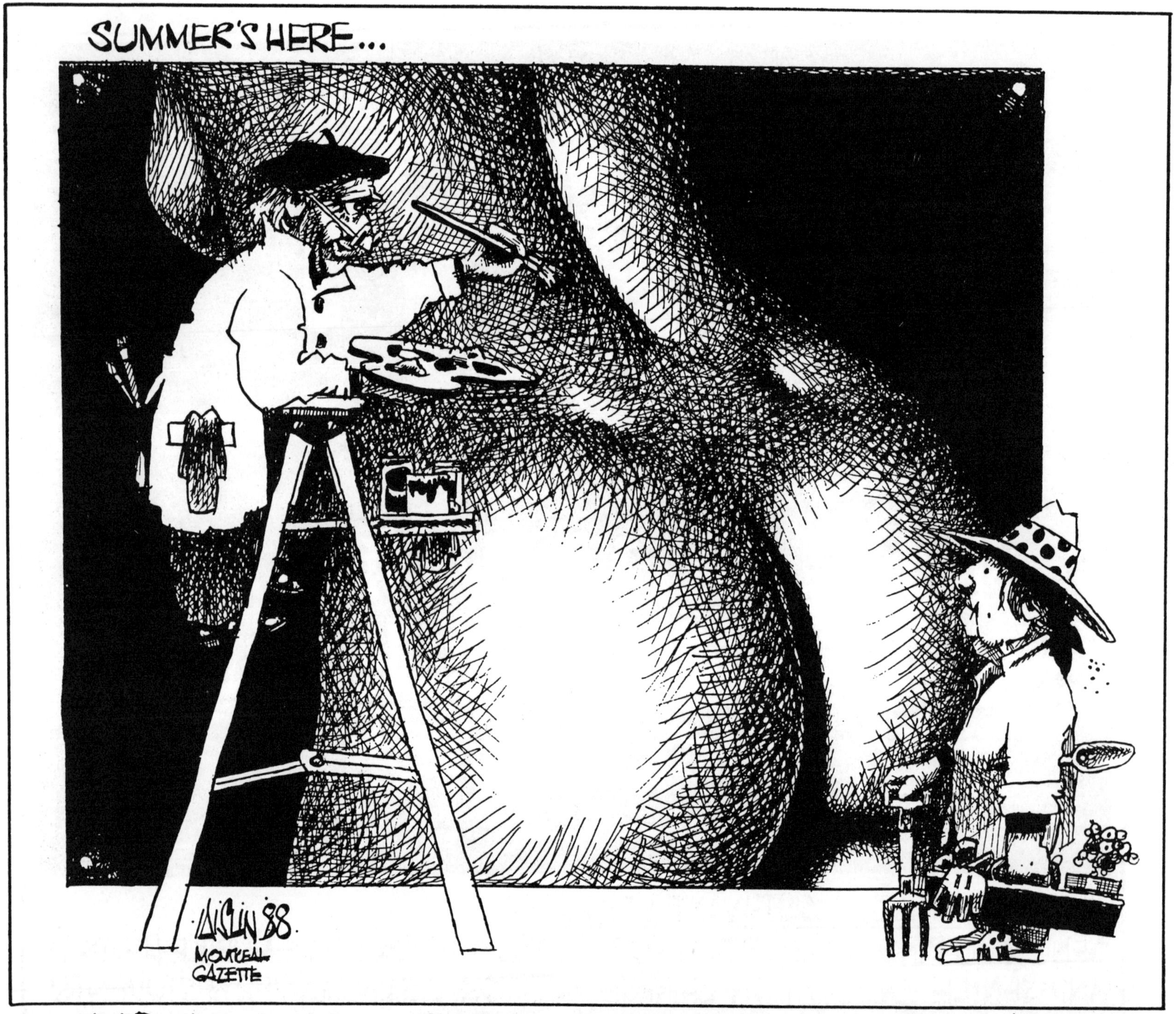

"QUITE FRANKLY, BEATRICE, GARDENING JUST DOESN'T DO IT FOR ME ANYMORE."

"WHAT BUGS YOU?"

Gazette readers were asked to submit their pet peeves to be illustrated.

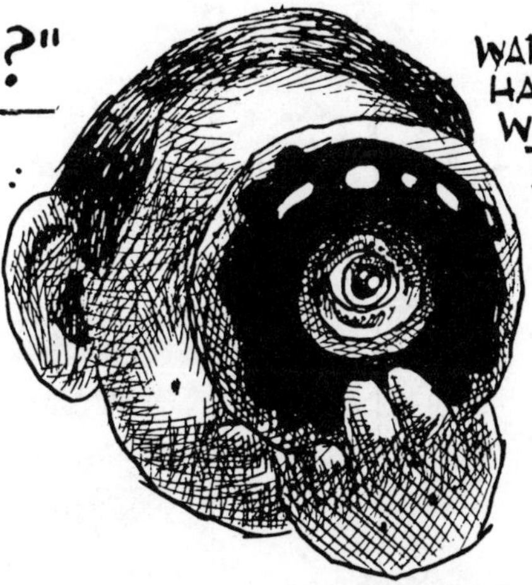

WARREN, AGE 3, HAD HIS MOM WRITE TO SAY THAT HE DOESN'T LIKE THE HOLES IN DONUTS.

"CHIP BAGS, HALF FULL OF AIR."

"ITS 7:30 A.M... THE SIREN GOES OFF TO HAVE ME MOVE MY CAR FOR THE SNOW-PLOWS... I'M MAKING LOVE..."

"MEN WHO LEAVE THE TOILET SEAT UP!"

"TRYING TO SHAVE AROUND THAT LITTLE HOLLOW BELOW THE NOSE."

"ALMOST BEING RUN OVER BY THOSE FAST LITTLE TANKS THAT PLOW THE SIDEWALKS!"

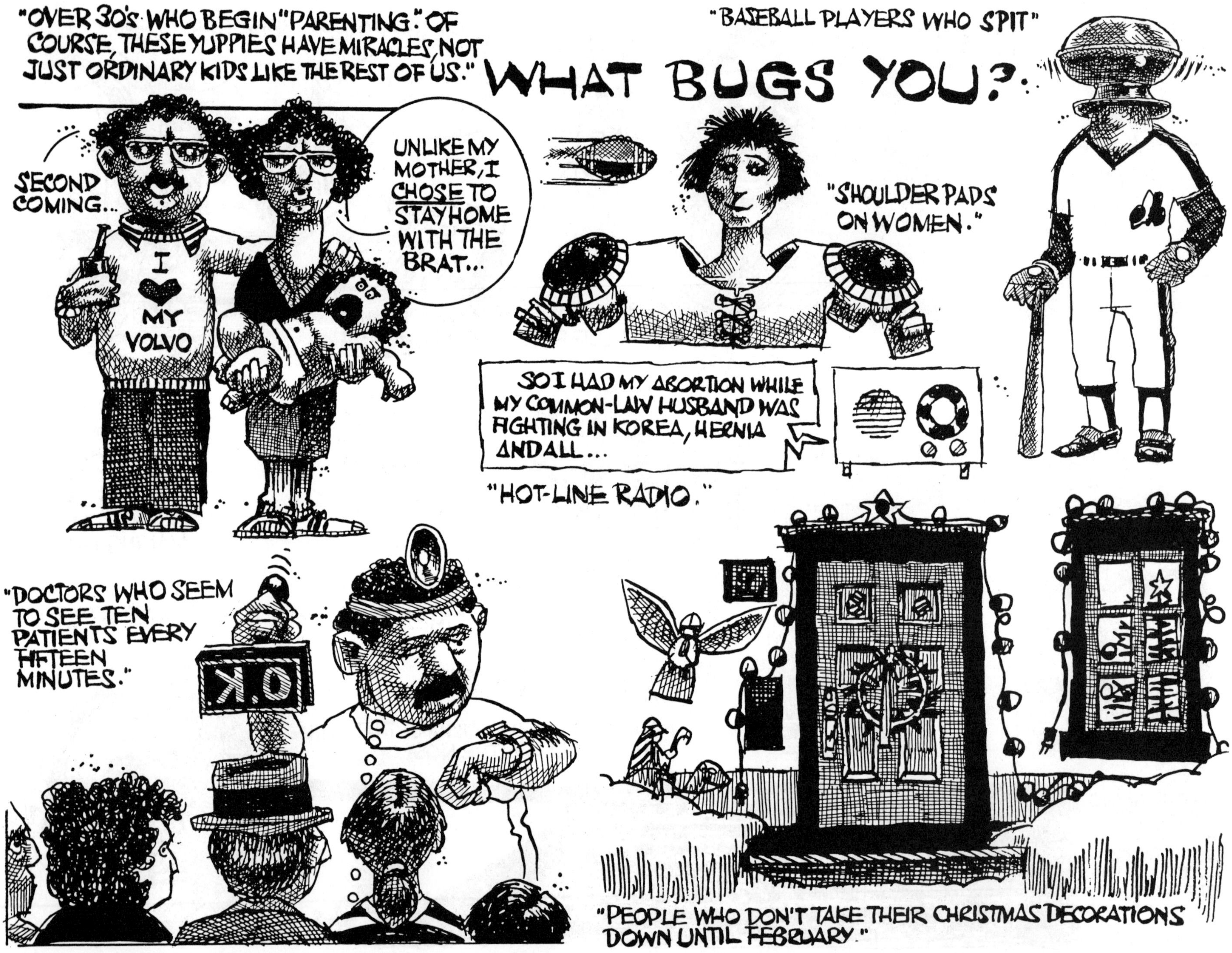
WHAT BUGS YOU?
"OVER 30's WHO BEGIN "PARENTING." OF COURSE, THESE YUPPIES HAVE MIRACLES, NOT JUST ORDINARY KIDS LIKE THE REST OF US."
SECOND COMING...
I ♥ MY VOLVO
UNLIKE MY MOTHER, I CHOSE TO STAY HOME WITH THE BRAT...
"BASEBALL PLAYERS WHO SPIT"
"SHOULDER PADS ON WOMEN."
SO I HAD MY ABORTION WHILE MY COMMON-LAW HUSBAND WAS FIGHTING IN KOREA, HERNIA AND ALL...
"HOT-LINE RADIO."
"DOCTORS WHO SEEM TO SEE TEN PATIENTS EVERY FIFTEEN MINUTES."
O.K
"PEOPLE WHO DON'T TAKE THEIR CHRISTMAS DECORATIONS DOWN UNTIL FEBRUARY."

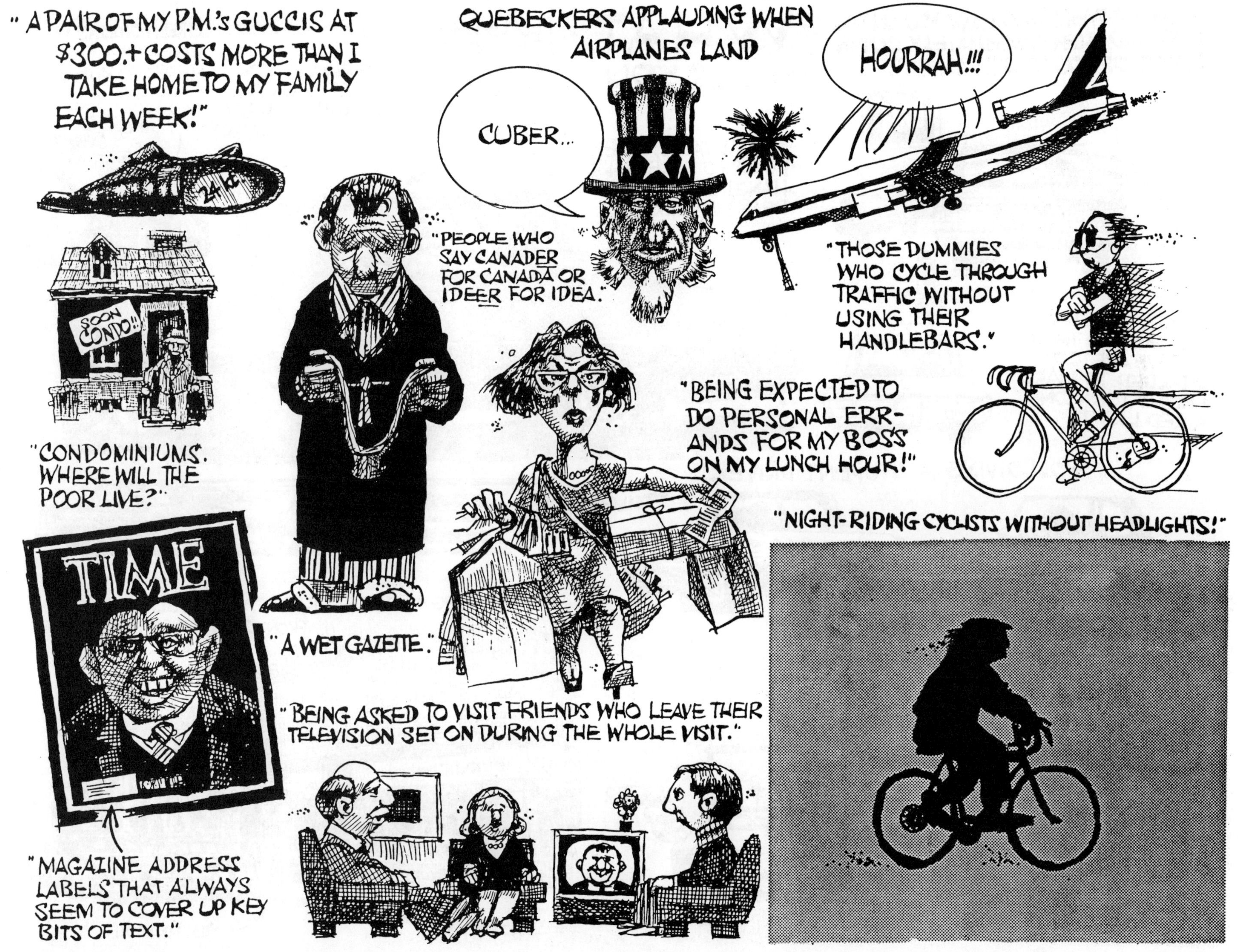

" A PAIR OF MY P.M.'s GUCCIS AT $300.+ COSTS MORE THAN I TAKE HOME TO MY FAMILY EACH WEEK!"
SOON CONDO!!
"CONDOMINIUMS. WHERE WILL THE POOR LIVE?"
TIME
"A WET GAZETTE."
"MAGAZINE ADDRESS LABELS THAT ALWAYS SEEM TO COVER UP KEY BITS OF TEXT."
"PEOPLE WHO SAY CANADER FOR CANADA OR IDEER FOR IDEA."
CUBER...
QUEBECKERS APPLAUDING WHEN AIRPLANES LAND
HOURRAH!!!
"THOSE DUMMIES WHO CYCLE THROUGH TRAFFIC WITHOUT USING THEIR HANDLEBARS."
"BEING EXPECTED TO DO PERSONAL ERR-ANDS FOR MY BOSS'S ON MY LUNCH HOUR!"
"BEING ASKED TO VISIT FRIENDS WHO LEAVE THEIR TELEVISION SET ON DURING THE WHOLE VISIT."
"NIGHT-RIDING CYCLISTS WITHOUT HEADLIGHTS!"

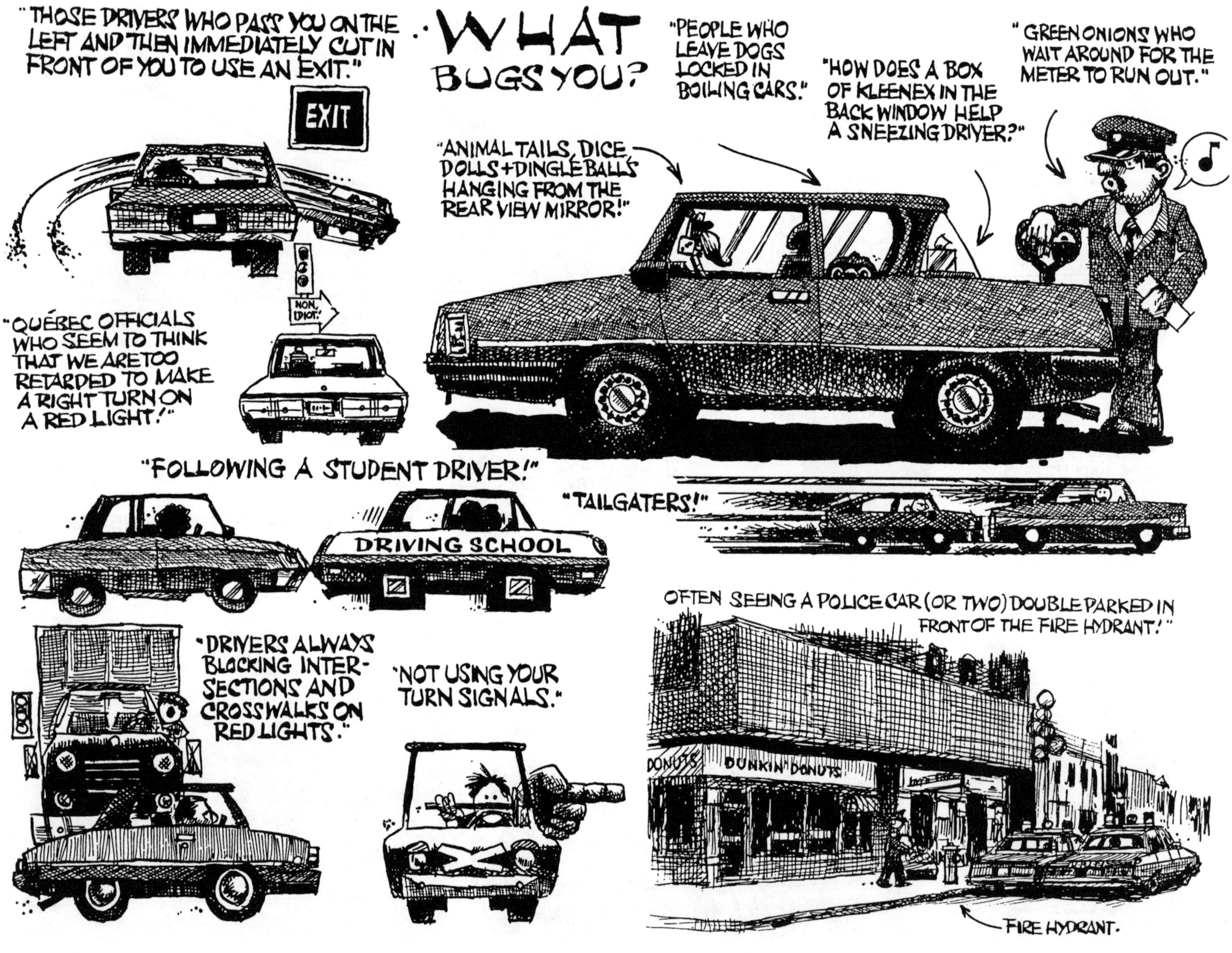
WHAT BUGS YOU?
"THOSE DRIVERS WHO PASS YOU ON THE LEFT AND THEN IMMEDIATELY CUT IN FRONT OF YOU TO USE AN EXIT."
EXIT
"PEOPLE WHO LEAVE DOGS LOCKED IN BOILING CARS."
"HOW DOES A BOX OF KLEENEX IN THE BACK WINDOW HELP A SNEEZING DRIVER?"
"GREEN ONIONS WHO WAIT AROUND FOR THE METER TO RUN OUT."
"ANIMAL TAILS, DICE, DOLLS + DINGLE BALLS HANGING FROM THE REAR VIEW MIRROR!"
"QUÉBEC OFFICIALS WHO SEEM TO THINK THAT WE ARE TOO RETARDED TO MAKE A RIGHT TURN ON A RED LIGHT!"
NON IDIOT
"FOLLOWING A STUDENT DRIVER!"
DRIVING SCHOOL
"TAILGATERS!"
"DRIVERS ALWAYS BLOCKING INTERSECTIONS AND CROSSWALKS ON RED LIGHTS."
"NOT USING YOUR TURN SIGNALS."
OFTEN SEEING A POLICE CAR (OR TWO) DOUBLE PARKED IN FRONT OF THE FIRE HYDRANT!"
DONUTS
DUNKIN' DONUTS
FIRE HYDRANT.

"RELATIVES WHO INSIST THAT YOU NOT GO TO ANY TROUBLE OVER THEM."
JUST YOUR GUILT WILL DO!!
"PRICE STICKERS THAT COVER THE DIRECTIONS ON DRUG BOTTLES AND OTHER CONTAINERS."
DIRECTIONS
WARN
$14.85
AND ON THE 7th DAY, BOB DYLAN RESTED.
"MY PARENTS GIVING ME OLD, OLD ROCK+ROLL RECORDS."
THE BAND
BANCO QUICKO
LEDGER
"THE MISS BLACK AMERICA CONTEST. IMAGINE THE HOWLS OF OUTRAGE IF THERE WERE A MISS WHITE AMERICA CONTEST!"
PEANUT BUTTER
MUSTARD
"PEOPLE WHO USE THE SAME KNIFE FOR THE BUTTER DISH, JAM JAR, HONEY POT, ETC."
"USELESS PENNIES."
"PEOPLE DOING THEIR MONTHLY BANKING AT CASH MACHINES."
"PEOPLE TELLING YOU WHAT IS GOING TO HAPPEN NEXT IN A MOVIE."
NOW SHE'LL HIT'M WITH A HAMMER!..
"THE C.B.C.'s OBSESSION WITH THE BLUE JAYS."
"...THAT TOO MANY PEOPLE AREN'T LUCKY ENOUGH TO HAVE OTHERS TO SHARE XMAS WITH AS I DO."
AARGH!
BLAT!!
"ANOTHER SICK AISLIN CARTOON!"

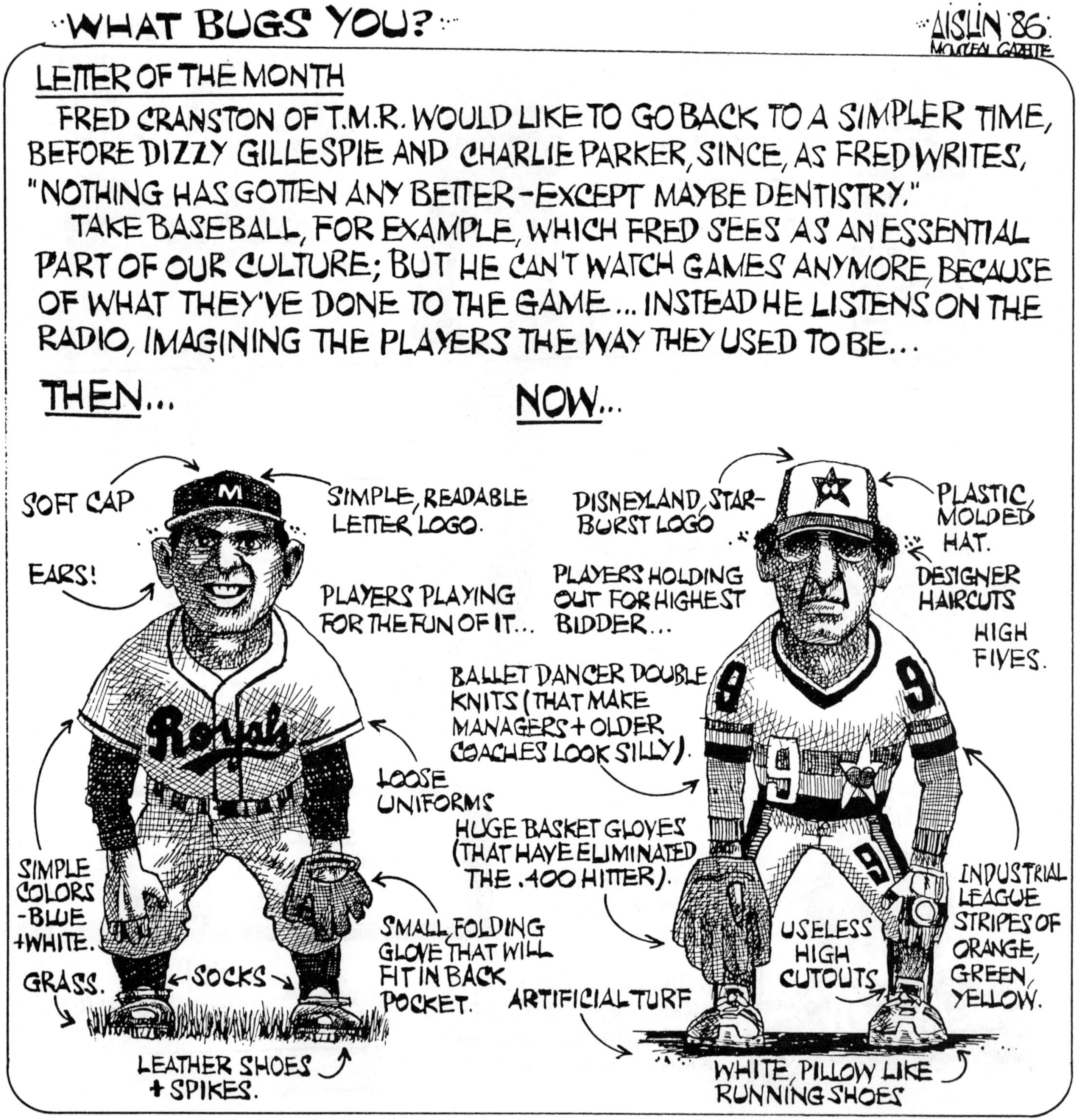
WHAT BUGS YOU?
AISLIN '86
MONTREAL GAZETTE
LETTER OF THE MONTH
FRED CRANSTON OF T.M.R. WOULD LIKE TO GO BACK TO A SIMPLER TIME, BEFORE DIZZY GILLESPIE AND CHARLIE PARKER, SINCE, AS FRED WRITES, "NOTHING HAS GOTTEN ANY BETTER - EXCEPT MAYBE DENTISTRY."
TAKE BASEBALL, FOR EXAMPLE, WHICH FRED SEES AS AN ESSENTIAL PART OF OUR CULTURE; BUT HE CAN'T WATCH GAMES ANYMORE, BECAUSE OF WHAT THEY'VE DONE TO THE GAME... INSTEAD HE LISTENS ON THE RADIO, IMAGINING THE PLAYERS THE WAY THEY USED TO BE...
THEN...
NOW...
SOFT CAP
SIMPLE, READABLE LETTER LOGO.
M
EARS!
PLAYERS PLAYING FOR THE FUN OF IT...
Royals
LOOSE UNIFORMS
SIMPLE COLORS - BLUE + WHITE.
SMALL, FOLDING GLOVE THAT WILL FIT IN BACK POCKET.
GRASS.
SOCKS
LEATHER SHOES + SPIKES.
DISNEYLAND STAR-BURST LOGO
PLASTIC, MOLDED HAT.
PLAYERS HOLDING OUT FOR HIGHEST BIDDER...
DESIGNER HAIRCUTS
HIGH FIVES.
BALLET DANCER DOUBLE KNITS (THAT MAKE MANAGERS + OLDER COACHES LOOK SILLY).
9
HUGE BASKET GLOVES (THAT HAVE ELIMINATED THE .400 HITTER).
INDUSTRIAL LEAGUE STRIPES OF ORANGE, GREEN, YELLOW.
USELESS HIGH CUTOUTS
ARTIFICIAL TURF
WHITE, PILLOW LIKE RUNNING SHOES

AISLIN AT SPRING TRAINING
WELL, FLOYD, BOB GIBSON HAD TO WORK OUT, SANDY KOUFAX HAD TO WORK OUT...
UNLIKELY INTERVIEW
SEEMS ABSURD, DON'T IT, PAYING US ALL THAT CASH JUST TO THROW A BALL. ALMOST AS ABSURD AS PAYING YOU GOOD MONEY TO WRITE ABOUT IT...
SMITH 28
17
36
AN EARLY BIRD IN NIRVANA.

...BUT ONLY AMATEURS USE THE E.R.A... I ADD UP THE NUMBER OF HITS ALLOWED, WALKS (x1.3), AND HOME RUNS (x3), THEN SUBTRACT TOTAL K'S AND DIVIDE THAT BY INNINGS PITCHED. THEN...
WHAT IS THIS MANIAC TALKING ABOUT?
NRA
Walgreen's
101
MICHEL MOUSE
Party!
JESSE
YEP... IT'S SNOWIN' BACK HOME HEE... HEE...
MANY TOURISTS FROM HOLLYWOOD IN LAUDERDALE COME UP TO WEST PALM WITH THE YANKEES.
CAMERAMEN ARE ALWAYS VOTED TO BE "THE WORST DRESSED" IN CAMP...
SPORTS WRITER-POTENTIAL RIMBAUD?
PHOTOGRAPHER-POTENTIAL RAMBO...

A SURE BET
GUYS WITH HIGH NUMBERS WON'T BE MAKING THE TEAM THIS YEAR
73
PEREZ
THE BIG, BAD YANKEES ARRIVE BY BUS FOR A GAME WITH THE EXPOS...
YANKE
ENOUGH AUTOGRAPHS!
CONTRASTS
6'10" PITCHING PROSPECT AND A 5' AND A PINCH COACH...
ROWE
1
EASY NOW, GRAMPS... WANT A PROGRAMME?
ITS TERRIBLE FOR THE GAME, THIS PETE ROSE BUSINESS!
BASEBALL TODAY at 1:30
90
SPRING TRAINING
SHUTTLE TO DOG TRACK
AISLIN '89
MONTREAL GAZETTE

SPORTS…

Super Bowl Sunday.

"...CRANSTON BREAKS THROUGH THE LINE INTO HIS KITCHEN, TAKING A PERFECT PASS FROM HIS TERRIFIC WIFE, WHO SOMETIMES WONDERS HOW IT MIGHT HAVE BEEN HAD SHE MARRIED THAT OTHER SENSITIVE GUY WHO ALWAYS WANTED TO TAKE HER OUT TO THE BALLET AND STUFF!"

BUT DAD, WHY DIDN'T THOSE TORIES DISOWN SINC STEVENS AND HIS KIND AS QUICKLY AS THEY DID BEN?
WE STILL LOVE BEN
AISLIN 88.
MONTREAL GAZETTE

AISLIN 88
MONTREAL GAZETTE

AMERIMOOD
Pharmaceuticals
ADVERTISEMENT
DO YOU WANT TO LOOK LIKE BEN?
ASK YOUR M.D. FOR DETAILS
AMERIMOOD
Pharmaceuticals
I DON'T THINK SO, PERKINS...
AISLIN 88
MONTREAL GAZETTE

"AND LET ME SAY, MR. FRANCIS, YOU CERTAINLY APPEAR TO KNOW YOUR STUFF."

OTTAWA AND THE ELECTION…

FEATURING SOME of SINC'S I·N·F·A·M·O·U·S ROUTINES!!
CHRIST COIN TRICKS
KITING BIG CHEQUES
PAY MY LAWYERS AND I PROMISE NOT TO SQUEAL
WHAT'S 2 MILLION?
HOW TO MILK A BEAVER
PORKY MULDOON PRODUCTIONS PROUDLY PRESENTS
PC
AISLIN 97. MONTREAL GAZETTE
ADDITIONAL ACTS
MILA AND THE HOLT-RENFREWETTES
ROCH AND ROLL
WILD CAGED TUNA
COATES BOTTOMLESS
SUZANNE'S LIMO HIGH WIRE ACT
BISSONNETTE'S B.B.Q. CHICKENS
THE $INC $TEVENS CIRCUS!
MERCIFULLY CANCELLED

ADVICE FOR JOE CLARK...IF YOU'VE GOT IT, FLAUNT IT!

BUT WOULD YOU LET YOUR CHILD MARRY A CARNEY OR A CROSBIE?

NEWS ITEM: SHEILA COPPS TO BE SHADOW CRITIC
OF ENVIRONMENT MINISTER LUCIEN BOUCHARD.
TABARNOUCHE!
AISLIN 89
MONTREAL GAZETTE

Terrible drought in Western Canada.

BUT PERRIN JUST DOESN'T LOOK LIKE A WARMONGERING PEON OF THE MILIT-ARY-INDUSTRIALISTS!
NERVE GAS
CLEARASIL
COLONEL WIMP?
AISLIN '88
MONTREAL GAZETTE

"THE GOOD NEWS IS THAT ONLY ONE OF THEM CAN BE PRIME MINISTER."

Federal election is called.

A new conservative mood in traditionally liberal Quebec.

BOB'S NEUTRAL...
J'SUIS NEUTRE...
AISLIN 88
MONTREAL GAZETTE

ABOARD THE CAMPAIGN PLANE...
McPRESS
SO, NOW BRIAN McHAPPY CLAIMS HE STARTED OUT AS A LAD SLINGING HAMBURGERS IN BAIE COMEAU?
SURE...
McPRESS
I SUPPOSE THAT WAS WHEN HE WASN'T BUSY BEING A TRUCKER? OR SINGING FOR THE YANKEE TOWN BOSSES FOR $50.00??
...WHICH WAS PROBABLY $5.00...
AISLIN 88
MONTREAL GAZETTE

OKAY! OKAY! PERHAPS FREE TRADE WON'T BE THE GREATEST THING SINCE SLICED BREAD!!!... And, besides, Marie, it's been a week and a half...
AISLIN 88
MONTREAL GAZETTE

John Turner is a clear winner in the debates.

WE'RE RIDIN' HIGH NOW, JOHN! BUT HOW'RE WE GONNA PAY FOR SOME FUEL?
JEEZ, I DON'T KNOW! GO BACK AND GET SOME PRESS GUYS TO WHIZ IN THE TANK!
AISLIN 88
MONTREAL GAZETTE

"NO, BRIAN, LET MARGARET ATWOOD AND MEL HURTIG PRATTLE ON ALL THEY WANT ABOUT ECONOMIC AND CULTURAL SOVEREIGNTY. LIP GLOSS WILL SELL FREE TRADE IN KAMLOOPS!"

MULRONEY'S RICH...CROSBIE'S RICH...SO THEY WANT FREE TRADE FOR A REASON!
RESTAUR
EMILE BERTRAND
AISLIN '88

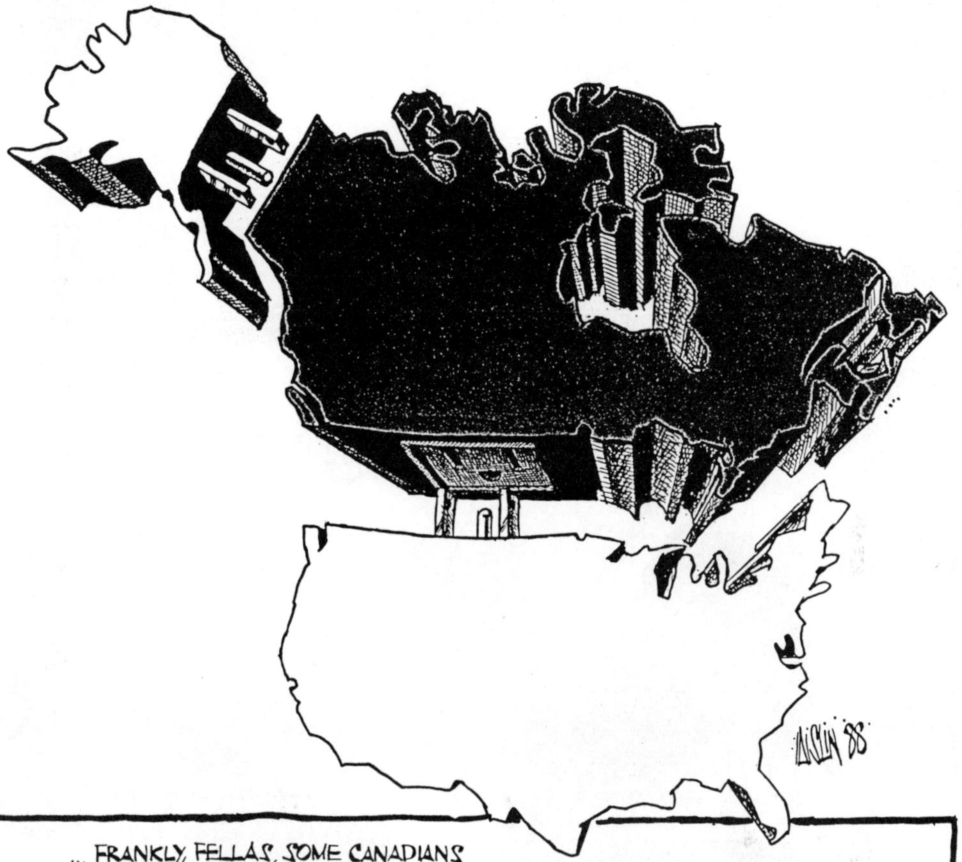
AISLIN '88

ONE CANADIAN AND TEN AMERICAN BUSINESSMEN DISCUSS FREE TRADE...
... FRANKLY, FELLAS, SOME CANADIANS DON'T SEEM TO TRUST US!
AISLIN '88 MONTREAL GAZETTE

C'MON BRIAN, YOU'RE NOT SCARING THEM!
AISLIN '88
MONTREAL GAZETTE

ANGELS
ANGELS
D.C.
U.S.
AISLIN 88
MONTREAL GAZETTE

Tories win the election and Free Trade.

YES, YES... YOU DID WELL, BRIAN...
MOVE!
AISLIN 88
MONTREAL GAZETTE

MR. SPEAKER, DISCIPLINING POORER PEOPLE IS AN INHERENT PART OF ANY CONSERVATIVE'S PHILOSOPHY... CAN I HELP IT IF SOME TORIES LIKE TO WATCH?

...COULDN'T YOU GALS JUST GO-PLAY IN HOLT-RENFREW AND SORT THIS THING OUT?

A BULLONEY MIX…

"BRIAN," DALTON SAID, "WE'RE GOING TO HAVE TO FIND YOU A BELIEVABLE AND PALATABLE ROLE MODEL...
DOUGH BOY
AISLIN '87
MONTREAL GAZETTE

OUR POSITION ON THAT IS CLEAR...
AISLIN 88
MONTREAL GAZETTE

A TORY T.V. NETWORK?...
NEWS
TODAY, THE COUNTRY WAS STRONG, FIRM, VIRILE... AND I WAS O.K. TOO...
WEATHER
MONEY WILL CONTINUE TO RAIN ON BAIE-COMEAU...

BAIE COME
I'M SAD TO SAY TRUDEAU IS RESPONSIBLE ... WHATEVER YOUR PROBLEM
Madame Tussaud's
ITS VERY REALISTIC...
OH? I FIND IT WAX-LIKE
THAT'S WHAT I MEANT...
PRIME MINISTER of the CANADAS
AISLIN 89
MONTREAL GAZETTE

HEH, HEH...IS ALLRIGHT?
S'ALLRIGHT...
AISLIN 88
MONTREAL GAZETTE

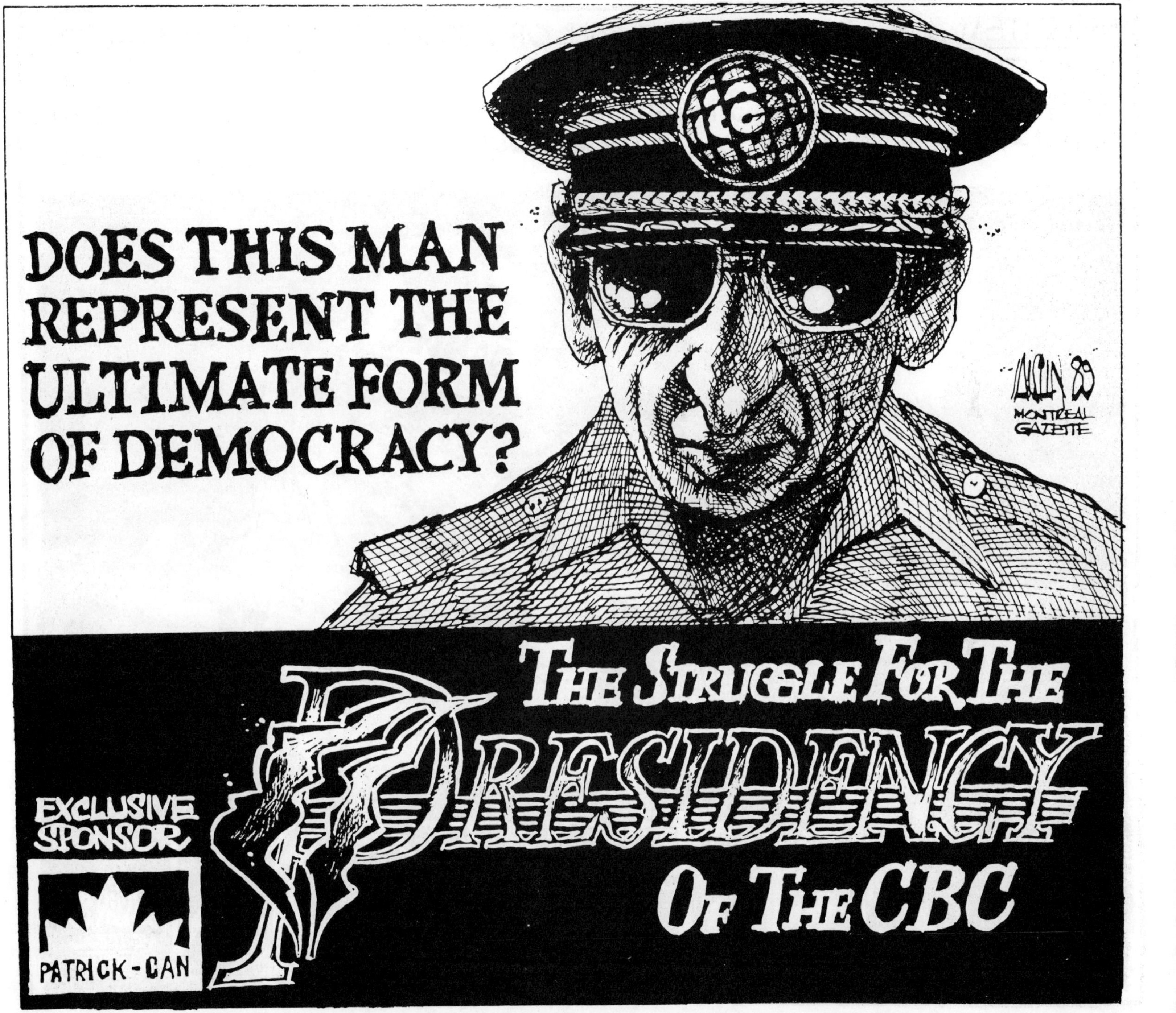

DOES THIS MAN REPRESENT THE ULTIMATE FORM OF DEMOCRACY?
MONTREAL GAZETTE
THE STRUGGLE FOR THE PRESIDENCY OF THE CBC
EXCLUSIVE SPONSOR
PATRICK-CAN

NEWS ITEM: A MACLEAN'S-DECIMA POLL OF 1,500 PEOPLE WOULD SEEM TO INDICATE THAT THE MOST SEXUALLY ACTIVE CANADIAN IS A MALE, AGED BETWEEN 25 AND 34, WHO MAKES OVER $40,000.00 A YEAR-BUT VOTED N.D.P.-AND LIVES COMMON-LAW SOMEWHERE IN RURAL NEWFOUNDLAND!
I ♥ GANDER
OBSESSION
AISLIN 88
MONTREAL GAZETTE

WHAT A WEEK COMING UP!
→ LES CANADIENS VS. THE BRUINS...
→ THE FLAMES VS. THE OILERS...
→ NEWFOUNDLAND VS. ST. PIERRE & MIQUELON...
AISLIN '88
MONTREAL GAZETTE

THE MEECH LAKE MONSTER
AISLIN '88
MONTREAL GAZETTE

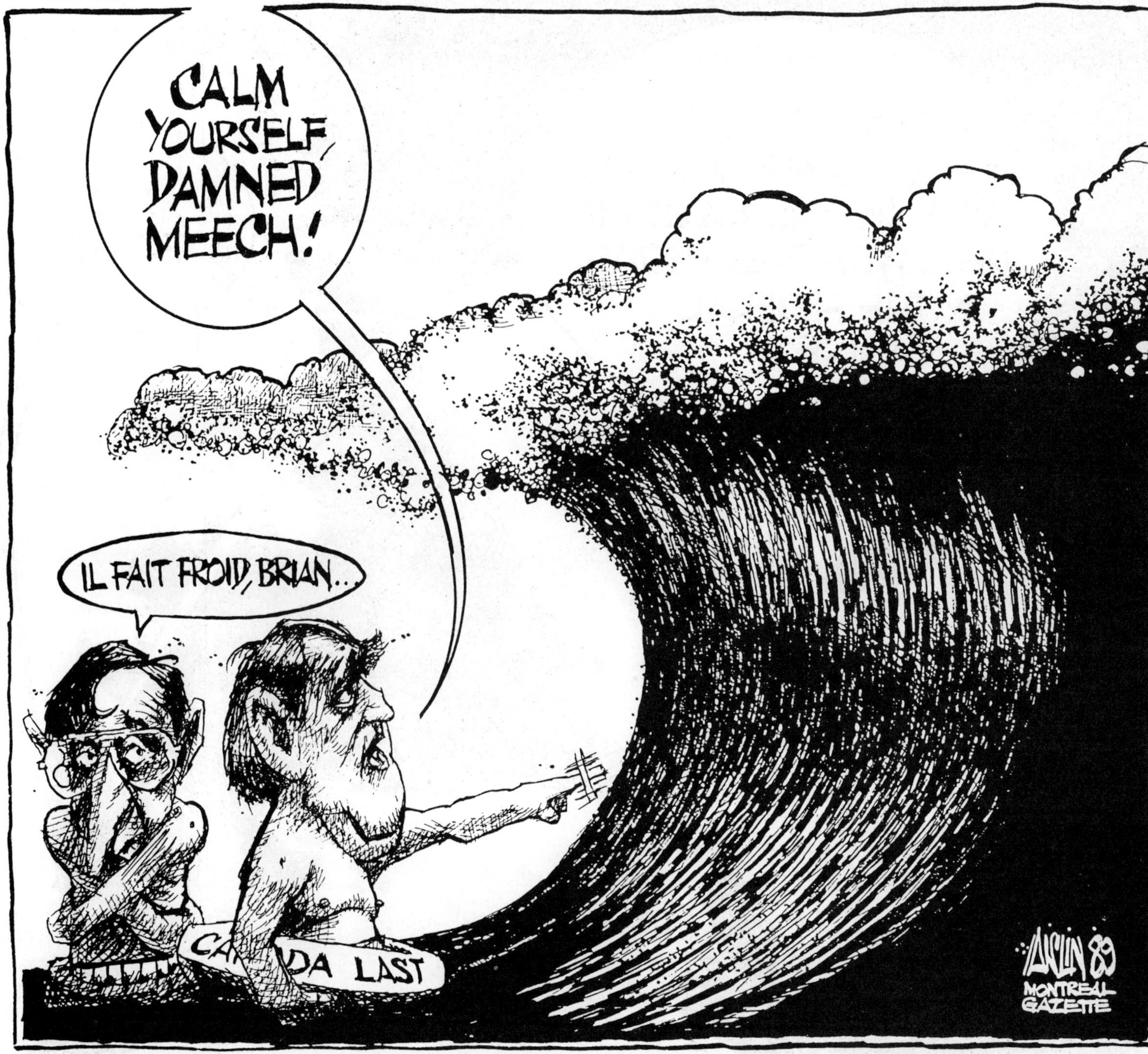
CALM YOURSELF, DAMNED MEECH!
IL FAIT FROID, BRIAN...
CANADA LAST
AISLIN 89
MONTREAL GAZETTE

Priests jailed in Newfoundland.

The United Church gay debate.

"…AND, OTHER THAN ME HAVING QUITE A GAY OLD TIME AT MS. SPONGEDILL'S WHITE WINE AND CRUMPET SOCIAL LAST FRIDAY, THE FLOCK NEEDN'T WORRY."

Ed Broadbent retires.

ED'S SO CUTE...HE'S GOOD FOR ANOTHER FIVE MINUTES OF THIS NONSENSE...THEN HE'LL HAVE TO FIND A SMOKE-FILLED BACK ROOM SOMEWHERE...
LUCILLE
AISLIN 89
MONTREAL GAZETTE

AISLIN '89
MONTREAL
GAZETTE

Ye Budget
© GLOBAL TELEVISION
AISLIN '89

AISLIN '89
MONTREAL GAZETTE

Quebec police can't find hijacked Greyhound bus.

QUEBEC…

CONTRACT
ZOOKEEP
MORE… BRING MORE… PLEASE.
TRUDEAU HE AIN'T..
AISLIN 89
MONTREAL GAZETTE

NEWS ITEM: CLEVER 'LA FRANCOPHONIE' ORGANIZERS DRUG PIGEONS TO PREVENT THEIR DUMPING ON OPENING CEREMONIES...
SALUT, BRO... AS-TU DES LUDES?
AISLIN '87
MONTREAL GAZETTE

Hydro-Québec blames the sun for power outages.

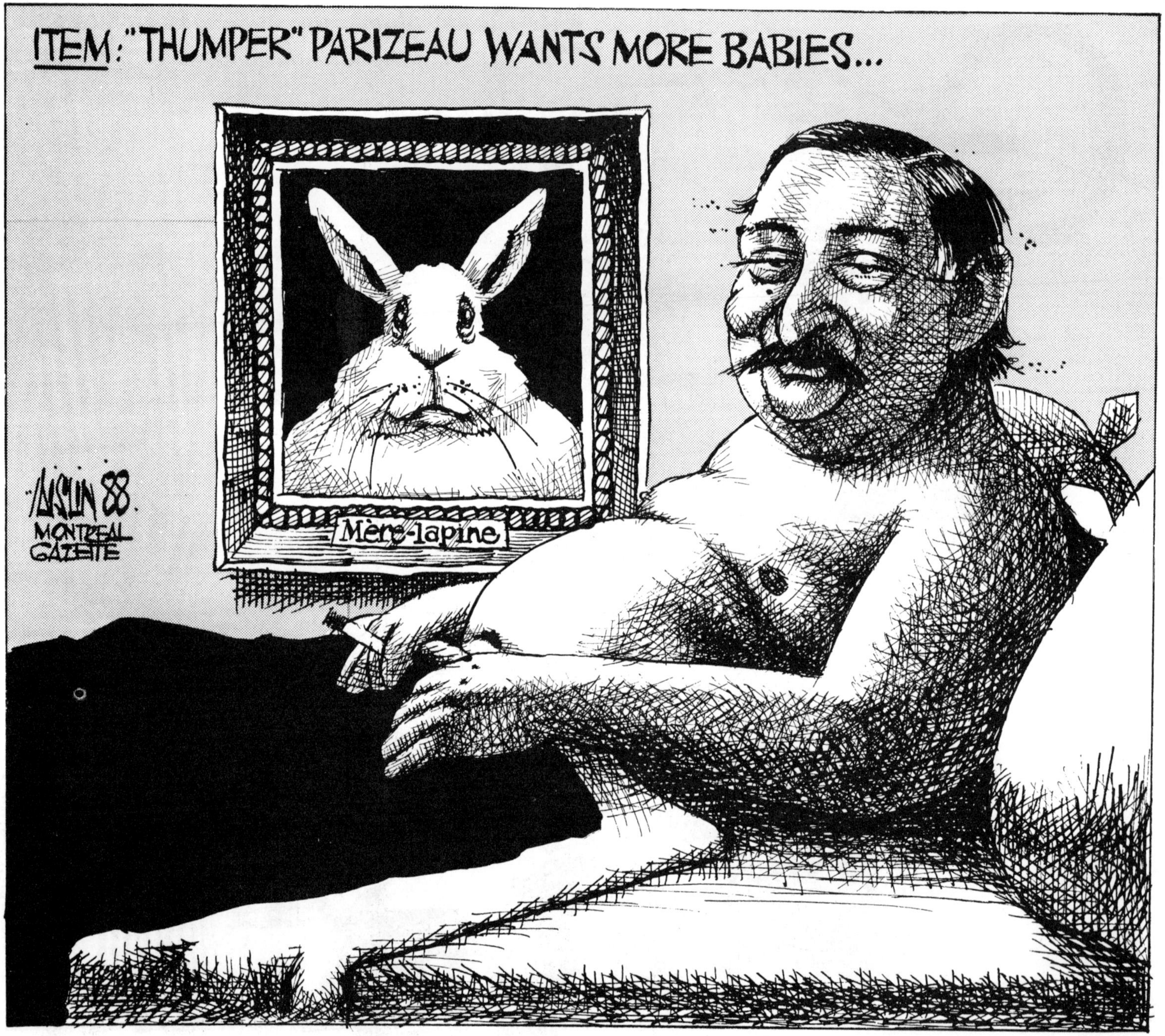
ITEM: "THUMPER" PARIZEAU WANTS MORE BABIES...
Mère-lapine
AISLIN 88
MONTREAL GAZETTE

NEWS ITEM: FRANCOPHONE LEADERS TO MEET AT LUXURIOUS CLUB MED...
HANDS UP! BABY, HANDS UP!
AISLIN '89
MONTREAL GAZETTE

THE TAIL THAT WAGS THE DOG!...

BOOBIE…

HMMM...
178 OVER 101...
MILK
AISLIN '89 MONTREAL GAZETTE

WE THOUGHT THE AMERICAN TOURISTS MIGHT LIKE IT...
CHEF

GROUNDHOG'S DAY...
IS IT SAFE TO COME OUT AND GO HOME NOW?
AISLIN '89 MONTREAL GAZETTE

POLLS SHOW ME TO BE THE MOST LOVED PREMIER IN ALL OF CANADA...
...AMONGST THE CARICATURISTS.
AISLIN 89
MONTREAL GAZETTE

THE UNIQUE QUEBEC THREE-PRONGED PLUG...

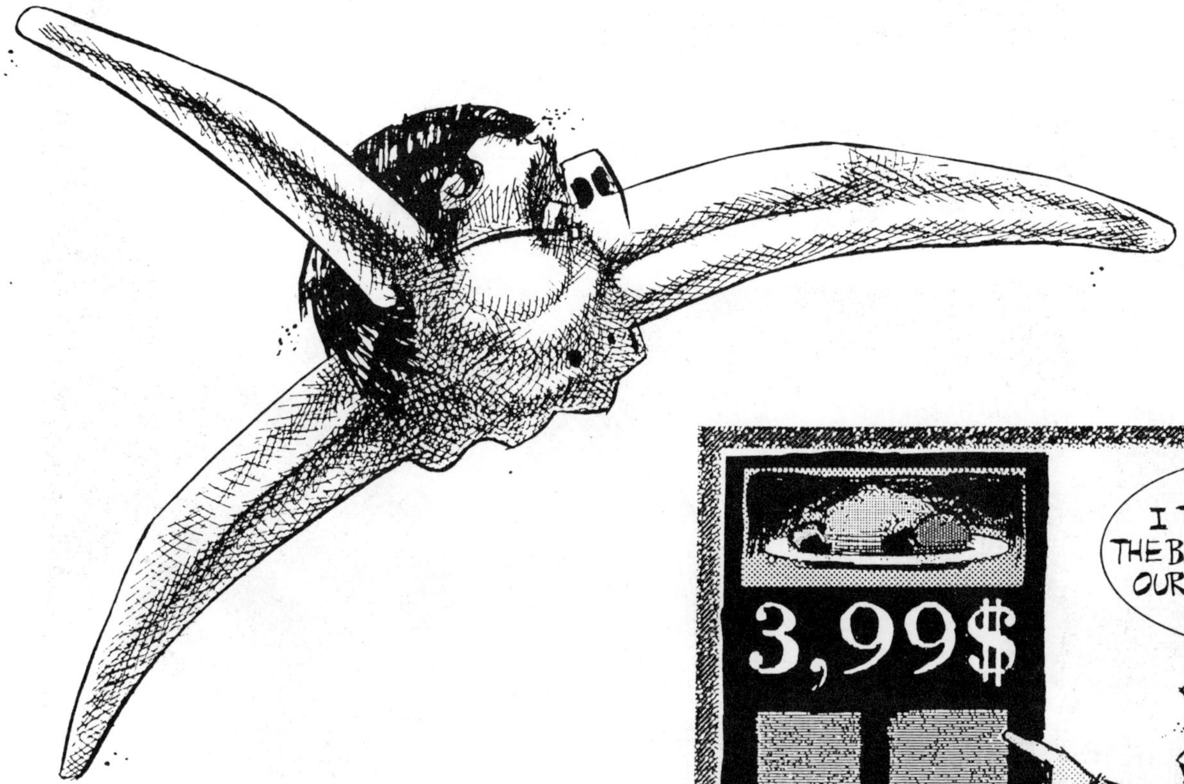

Cabinet minister falsely accuses Eaton('s) of having fat sales ladies who only speak English.

OUTSIDE, INSIDE...
SOYEZ RAISONNABLE, MONSIEUR ED! YOUR BILINGUAL SIGNS ARE A DISTINCT THREAT TO QUEBEC'S FRAGILE CULTURE!
UNLIKE MY NEW NEIGHBORS', I SUPPOSE?
onald's
BURG
KIN
BIENVENUE!/WELCOME!
CHEZ ED'S
PLAT DU JOUR/DAILY SPECIAL
Depuis/since 1930
Livraison Gratuite/Free Delivery
KING
AISLIN 88
MONTREAL GAZETTE

Cabinet Minister Claude Ryan is handed the Anglo portfolio.

ANGLOS…

Quebec's Anglos start playing a less passive role as their rights erode.

WHERE'S THE ANGLO PRIDE IN WHAT OUR CULTURE HAS PRODUCED?
AISLIN '89 MONTREAL GAZETTE
NORTH AMERICA'S BEST CHESS PLAYER...
ONE OF THE WORLD'S GREAT JAZZ ARTISTS...
CANADA'S FIRST WORLD CLASS AUTHOR...
OOO-OO... ANGST BAB-EE BLOOO-SSS
A POET-SONG WRITER WHO IS THE TOAST OF EUROPE...
A TWO-TIME GOLD OLYMPIC CHAMPION...
AND YES, OKAY, HIM TOO... BUT FIVE OUT OF SIX IS PRETTY GOOD!

LES ANGLOS DANS LES RUES...
Montreal cranes keep falling down.
Québec
HIP, HIP...
THIS IS STILL CANADA!
BILINGUAL SIGNS!
, FOREVER
ANGLO RIGHTS!
AISLIN '88
MONTREAL GAZETTE

Anglo cabinet ministers remain silent despite their constituents' concern over Bourassa's language policy.

DON'T QUIT, CLIFF... WE'LL COVER THE WHOLE DAMN WEST ISLAND WITH A TENT...
EVERYTHING WILL BE INSIDE!
N' BOB'LL LET US KEEP OUR LIMOS AND CELLULAR PHONES...
MONTREAL GAZETTE

YOU ARE WHAT YOU READ...
Muntreal Daily Noose
CITY TERRORIZED BY ALLI-Q ARSON!
DOG RAPES VERDUN FAMILY PAGE 3
TODAY
Snowdon orphaned widow receives FLQ threat
INFERNO
GILLES RHUME SEZ
Le Bistro Islandais!
Plat du jour RAGOÛT DE MULDOO
le joual de montréal
DROGUES, SEXE ET STEREOS...
SAINT JEAN-PAUL ROSE...
TÉLÉ-FLIRT!
"...UNE VENTE DE FEU CHEZ LES ANGLOS?"
AISLIN '89 MONTREAL GAZETTE
The Gazoo
Orr asks Decent majority to speak up somewhat
Much wringing of hands by our Anglophones
Hampsteadonians wringing their hands.
La Price
hier?
Rien de neuf aujourd'hui... peut-être demain...
Notre Outremont
Aucun
LE DÉVOREUR
Alliance-Québec
Le S.T.N.A.B.C.Q. propose qu'un comité soit établi
Les bureaucrates du S.S.N.A.R.S.S.T.N.D.U.U.A.NORT...

Much media speculation after a fire at Alliance-Québec headquarters.

Royal Orr hired by CJAD as talk-show host.

COMME NOUS AVONS DE L'EXPÉRIENCE EN TANT QUE MINORITÉ...
...À L'INTÉRIEUR D'UNE MAJORITÉ, QUÉBEC SERA AUSSI JUSTE...
...ENVERS SES MINORITÉS QUE LE CANADA L'A ÉTÉ AVEC NOUS!!
...BUT 28% OF FEDERAL CIVIL SERVANTS ARE FRENCH... LESS THAN 1% OF QUÉBEC'S FONCTIONNAIRES ARE ENGLISH...
WHACK!!
AISLIN 88
MONTREAL GAZETTE
Raciste...

NEWS ITEM: THE NEW MAYOR OF WESTMOUNT CLAIMS THAT HER CONSTITUENTS ARE THE MOST SOCIALLY CONSCIOUS, MORE CULTURALLY AWARE AND BETTER EDUCATED THAN ANY IN CANADA...
...WELL, WE ARE NICE TO OUR DOGS...
Twit College
Artiste
OGILVY FUND
NUDE MAID
AISLIN 87.

RIGHTS-R-RIGHTS-R-RIGHTS-R-RIGHTS...
HEH, HEH... HEH, HEH...
WHY ME, BRIAN?
TETLEY TEA! TETLEY TEA! BOYCOTT! BOYCOTT!
HMMM...A WOMAN OF SOME SPIRIT... THE TIME HAS COME, MY DEAR, TO TALK OF MANY THINGS...
OFF WITH THEIR HEADS!
WHAT? ME WORRY?
CURIOUSER AND CURIOUSER!
ZZZ...
THAT
WALRUS!
HOW'RE TRICKS?
BOB'S GOOD
WEINER
NOWELL
NICK
CUTLER
WESTMOUNT
CARPENTER FAINSTAT
CJAD
BLAIKIE
CIACCIA
AISLIN 86 MONTREAL GAZETTE
ALICE ATTENDS A MAD ANGLO TEA-PARTY...

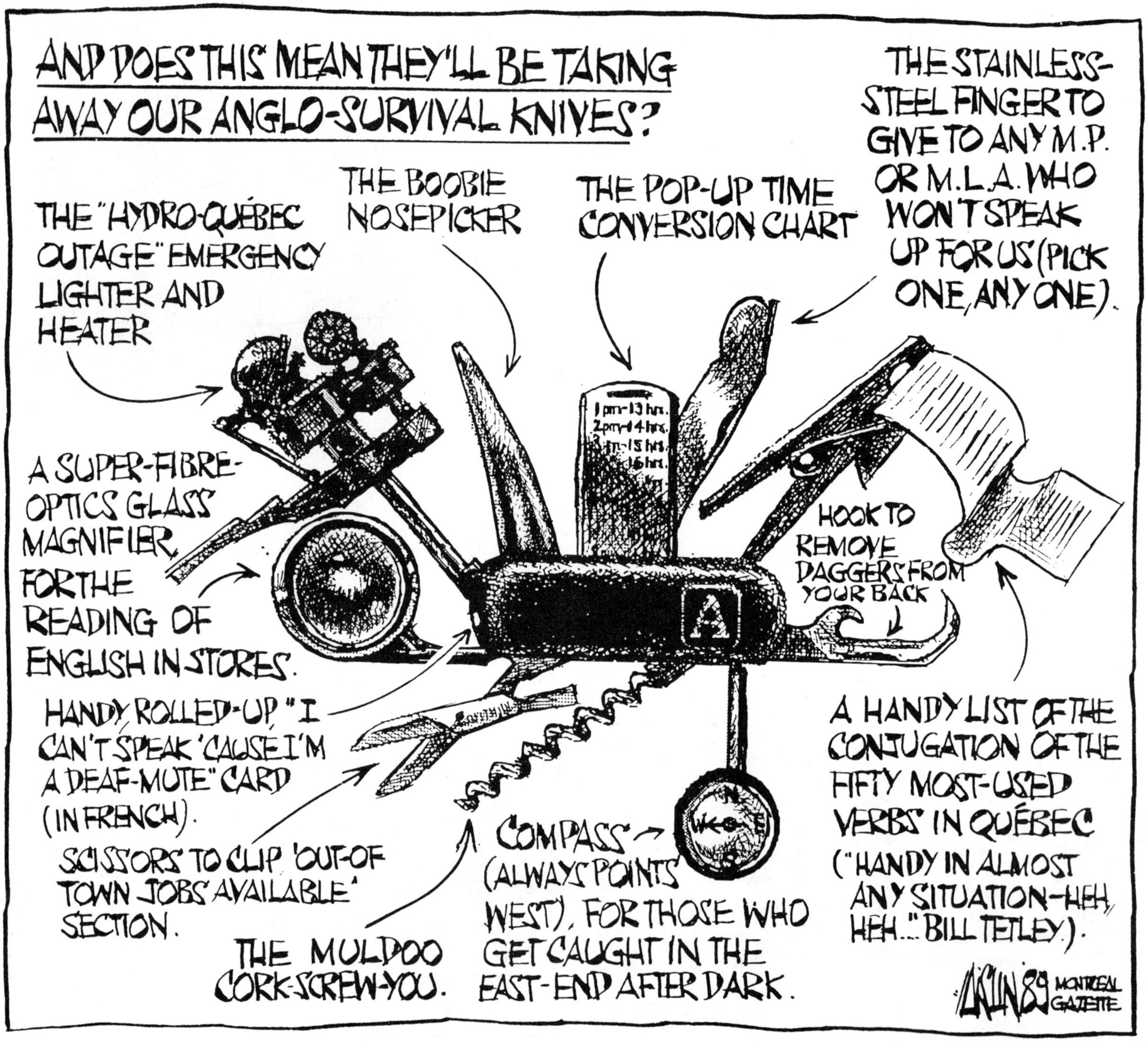
AND DOES THIS MEAN THEY'LL BE TAKING AWAY OUR ANGLO-SURVIVAL KNIVES?
THE "HYDRO-QUÉBEC OUTAGE" EMERGENCY LIGHTER AND HEATER
THE BOOBIE NOSEPICKER
THE POP-UP TIME CONVERSION CHART
THE STAINLESS-STEEL FINGER TO GIVE TO ANY M.P. OR M.L.A. WHO WON'T SPEAK UP FOR US (PICK ONE, ANY ONE).
A SUPER-FIBRE-OPTICS GLASS MAGNIFIER, FOR THE READING OF ENGLISH IN STORES.
HOOK TO REMOVE DAGGERS FROM YOUR BACK
HANDY ROLLED-UP "I CAN'T SPEAK 'CAUSE I'M A DEAF-MUTE" CARD (IN FRENCH).
SCISSORS TO CLIP 'OUT-OF TOWN JOBS AVAILABLE' SECTION.
COMPASS (ALWAYS POINTS WEST), FOR THOSE WHO GET CAUGHT IN THE EAST-END AFTER DARK.
A HANDY LIST OF THE CONJUGATION OF THE FIFTY MOST-USED VERBS IN QUÉBEC ("HANDY IN ALMOST ANY SITUATION-HEH, HEH..." BILL TETLEY).
THE MULDOO CORK-SCREW-YOU.
1pm-13 hrs.
2pm-14 hrs.
A
AISLIN 89 MONTREAL GAZETTE

BOOTYMAN
RINCE
AISLIN 89
MONTREAL GAZETTE.

SALUT, VIEUX... ÇA MARCHE?
PAS TROP MAL, TOI?
COMME D'HABITUDE. AS-TU VU LE MATCH AVEC LES BRUINS HIER SOIR?
NON...MOI, JE PRÉFÈRE LE BASEBALL, ET J'AI TRÈS HÂTE...
...AU MOIS DE FÉVRIER ET AU COMMENCEMENT DE L'ENTRAÎNEMENT ...UMM....
PRINTANIER?
OUI, PRINTANIER...
AISLIN '89 MONTREAL GAZETTE
THIS IS ABSURD, DANNY. NOBODY'S LISTENING.
YEAH... WELL NOT YET ANYWAY, BILL.

Parliament and the baseball season open on the same day.

The Lawn Jockey is the twentieth book by Terry Mosher, a.k.a. Aislin, the editorial-page cartoonist of *The Gazette* in Montreal.

Mosher, 46, was born in Ottawa. He attended fourteen schools in Montreal, Ottawa and Quebec City before graduating from the Quebec Ecole des beaux-arts in 1967. He began working for the Montreal *Star* and later moved over to *The Gazette*.

Aislin cartoons are syndicated throughout Canada and have appeared in many prominent publications around the world. The recipient of many awards, Mosher was the youngest person ever inducted into The Canadian News Hall of Fame, in 1985.

His proudest accomplishment, however, is being an eleven-year member of The Baseball Writers' Association of America. This gives him a vote for inductees to baseball's Hall of Fame in Cooperstown, N.Y. And, yes, he voted for Fergie Jenkins.

Mosher lives in downtown Montreal with his wife, two daughters and nine cats—seven at home, two in his *Gazette* studio.

Each year, a number of Canadian authors are asked to attend sponsored dinners, the proceeds of which go to young writers. This Aislin self-portrait was drawn in response to one of those evenings.